Livin

Esther de Waal lives in Herefordshire, close to the border between England and Wales, having returned to the countryside where she grew up. A sense of place has always been important and, after Cambridge, she became the first research student in the newly founded Department of Local History at Leicester. It was the buildings and the landscape that led to her monastic interest in the Benedictine, Cistercian and Celtic traditions. Her first interests now are her garden and her increasing number of grandchildren, but she also finds time to write, to take retreats and to travel – feeling a particular connection with South Africa.

The *Borders* series of small books is published in association with the Society of the Sacred Cross, an Anglican religious community, based at Tymawr, near Monmouth.

Other titles in the series include:

BORDERS

Living on the Border

Connecting Inner and Outer Worlds

Esther de Waal

CANTERBURY
PRESS
Norwich

© Esther de Waal 2001

First published in 2001 by The Canterbury Press Norwich
(a publishing imprint of Hymns Ancient & Modern Limited,
a registered charity)
St Mary's Works, St Mary's Plain
Norwich, Norfolk NR3 3BH

Esther de Waal has asserted her right under the
Copyright, Design and Patents Act, 1988, to be
identified as the Author of this Work

British Library Cataloguing in Publication Data

A catalogue record for this book is available
from the British Library

ISBN 1–85311–451–0

Typeset by Rowland Phototypesetting Ltd,
Bury St Edmunds, Suffolk
Printed in Great Britain by Biddles Ltd,
Guildford and King's Lynn

CONTENTS

BORDERS
SERIES INTRODUCTION

'Borderlands are ambiguous places in which different cultures and traditions meet, frontiers from which the new can open up.' Esther de Waal, *A World Made Whole*.

The inspiration for this series of short books comes from the Society of the Sacred Cross, an Anglican contemplative community situated at Tymawr (Welsh for 'big house') Convent near Monmouth, South Wales. Its position on the border between England and Wales, and on the boundary between the Welsh and English provinces of the Anglican Communion, has made the Society more aware of its ability to provide a meeting ground for people of different religious backgrounds and varied experiences of God.

From this awareness has arisen a recognition that pilgrims on the Christian journey often enter border country. Political events, cultural changes and developments in science and technology are some of the stimuli that daily challenge us to apply a Christian mind to a fast-moving world. In our personal lives, an unexpected change can suddenly occur and we find ourselves in an unfamiliar landscape, unsure of which direction to take next.

Titles in this series are written out of the author's extensive experience in his or her field and are offered as companions and guides to the various personal, practical, spiritual or philosophical frontiers we may be exploring.

*

For further details about the Society of the Sacred Cross, please contact:

The Society of the Sacred Cross
Tymawr Convent
Lydart
Monmouth NR25 4RN

INTRODUCTION

I have come back to live where I grew up. I have returned to the slower rhythms and the earth-linked textures of life on the Welsh Borders, a place which was a total contrast to life spent elsewhere, in a big university in the Midlands or an important cathedral city in the crowded South-east of England. As I root myself here I am finding that it is at once familiar and strange. This landscape has become my teacher, my mentor.

It takes time to realise this but I am beginning to realise just how profound an effect it has had on my life, on the way in which I approach time, people, situations and issues. I suppose that I might sum it up by saying that I have become aware of the continual movement of crossing over thresholds into the new, while still of course being part of what is left behind. It applies above all in my own life and in the emerging pattern that I discern now that I am (as my journalist son put it so magnificently) on the cusp of old age. But it has also influenced the way in which I look at situations, and how I relate to other people. As I try to sum it up, a whole galaxy of words starts to come tumbling out:

openness to change, ready and willing to move forward, living without defences rather than hiding behind barriers. In the end, if I were to find one single word that catches this sense of thresholds opening up into the new and the unknown, it would be transformation – and transformations, as William Countryman reminds us, 'are always at least a little scary'. To be transformed implies letting go of our control for a while in the hopeful expectation that something worthwhile can result. It means taking the risk that our old certainties might be replaced by a new way of seeing the world. Another word is conversion, not in the relatively easy sense of changing to religion, or from one denomination to another, but in the much more demanding sense of 'turning round', and 'discovering that there's a whole world out there that you hadn't really been aware of'.[1]

I can only learn from this border countryside landscape when I let its presence reveal itself to me gently, so that I begin to sense its patterns – those hill rhythms and water rhythms which had such a profound effect upon David Jones, the artist and poet, when he lived a few miles away at Capel-y-ffin in the Llanthony valley in the Black Mountains. In an autobiographical talk he said that in those years between 1924 and 1926, as he came to know the valley and the hills, he found that his work was influenced by the strong hill rhythms and the bright counter-rhythms of the water brooks. He found that there was no stillness in this landscape, but that here the movement of streams, wind, rain and cloud ceaselessly transform – in change which reveals the unchanging.[2]

Already I am being brought into a world where significant things are shown as images, and insight comes from shapes and patterns, from the visual rather than from the written word. Here I come face to face with what is elemental, both in my own self and in the world around. So although I began with the experience of a physical landscape I have been taken beyond that to explore successively the interplay of light and dark, of time and season as they alternate and move on, and my own life as it also moves forward. I consider how I am to embrace change in the context of the movement from birth to death, with its universal and inescapable stages. Am I willing to cross the threshold of new understanding by being open and receptive, not closed in and defensive? These questions also arise as I think not only about physical growth but also about growth into understanding and wisdom. The most profound threshold, however, remains that between the inner and the outer, between going deeper into the interior self and emerging to meet the world beyond the self without protective defences, as friend not as foe.

But, of course, a border landscape is not the only situation that allows one this particular experience. Ultimately, it is about a way of seeing that takes one beyond and outside what is immediately at hand and allows it to become a threshold beyond itself. It is a crossing over which will be totally specific to that person, that moment, that place. The top of a London bus is an admirable vantage spot for enjoying an urban skyline, noticing the pattern of rooftops, the domestic windows of upper floors that have resisted the development into shops and still retain delightful fenestration. Chimney pots are endless in their variety and inventiveness in the suburbs, of differing materials and styles, reminders of the domestic hearth and what it symbolized even though it may no longer be more than a memory. Tall factory chimneys can be as splendid as any church spire in the older industrial areas, and recall all the complexity of those early industrial ventures, which brought both suffering and success. Looking without judging is an art that can become a preliminary to opening up to new horizons.

The border country in which I find myself has brought me many fellow-companions whom I can summon to accompany me on my journey of exploration: the poets and the writers who flourished here; the monastic men and women, Celtic and Benedictine, who lived and prayed here; the saints and the angels who so richly inhabit the local region. So, although this is a most solitary journey, it is also one which is shared – and my hope is that it may be one that my readers are happy to make with me.

1

THE BORDER LANDSCAPE

Reading a landscape

I am now setting out to try to uncover or rediscover a whole world which lies around me, and to discover it in such a way that the exterior landscape might shape and mould the inner landscape. It is an exploration which I believe that I can best undertake by using the imagination in image and poetry and metaphor. As I turn to the land and to its poets and artists I want to make this an undertaking not only for myself but because I hope that my own specific encounter with a specific place may speak to each of my readers and give them images which they can relate to their own personal experience. This book comes out of a particular place but I hope that what it is speaking about has a wider application, with implications for people living in an urban environment or in a different culture. For it is not just about a rural situation of great beauty, but it is ultimately about making any place or any circumstance the threshold into the other, the new, the strange, and showing the image of difference, mystery, otherness at work in God's world.

Although my earliest childhood was spent in the Welsh border countryside, I had not then learnt how to read it or appropriate it. My father was an antiquarian of the old school and I owe to him my sense of history and my knowledge of medieval architecture. His approach was quintessentially that of a man fascinated by factual information of a most precise nature. He wanted to be able to date stones, whether in their natural state or shaped and used by local builders; but these were not living stones: they did not cry out. This was a world on which categories and labels were imposed, known through charts and charters, dates and land grants. These land charters with their concern for the giving and transferring of land between one owner and another, between one estate and another, encouraged an attitude of certainty and clarity about the past. From my mother I learnt another sort of certainty: certainty about the present, for she held very clear ideas about our neigh-bours across the border in Wales. Prejudice simplified her approach: the Welsh were small in stature, unreli-able in character, not to be trusted, and unworthy of any respect. 'Taffy was a Welshman, Taffy was a thief', the old jingle tripped only too easily off the tongue. They came to raid, crossing over into England to make inroads into our fair and pleasant land. There was not therefore any idea of giving and receiving, and doorways were shut, defrauding me of what, even as a small child, might have taught me to be receptive, ready to learn from the other. I had no sense of thresholds to cross, or borders to break; there was nothing to encourage openness or exploration.

Living on the border

Later on, married and with four young sons, my father presented us with a small cottage – two rooms up and two rooms downstairs, the traditional local pattern, with only one cold water tap and no inside lavatory. Two streams met here, the Cwm and the Greidol, and flowed over into a waterfall, where at the base lay a mass of huge rock slabs whose shape and position would gradually but dramatically change over the years under the impact of flood and storm. These swirling combinations of mud and silt and stone, continually different and new, gave me a metaphor for a natural configuration which maintains its form over time while yet retain-ing its ability to shape and adapt its configuration over the years. Since time immemorial streams have formed the boundaries between properties and settlements and very often, as here, they still carry their earliest Celtic or Welsh names. But even though the stream names might be Welsh, the village name was Saxon, though the church was the proud possessor in the sixteenth century of the Great Welsh Bible, the first Bible to be translated into Welsh by William Morgan in 1588. A mile or two away the neighbouring tiny church of Llangua, which can date its origins to a sixth-century Celtic saint, lies geographically in Wales while yet remaining in the Church of England.

Any neat demarcation, whether religious, economic or cultural, has little meaning in a border countryside such as this. This border has never been rigid, a young Monmouth farmer said recently – a Welshman who did well on the hills would look over the border and think of moving to the other side.

So when I now went walking along the stretch of Offa's Dyke which ran only a few miles away, I came to know afresh the world that had earlier delighted my father. He had told me the heroic story of Offa and his eighth-century ambitions, the man who dominated the whole of Britain between 757 and 795, a contemporary and almost an equal of Charlemagne. But that was now something of the historic past. A military frontier had become a pastoral border, with visible differences certainly and one could see that pattern written on the land itself. But it was now a place where two worlds met. I felt that I was looking beyond political ambition and military conquest. Of course I could see those differences: they were written into the pattern of the landscape. There was Wales on the west side, a country of mountains and scattered settlements, bare stretches of hillside covered with sheep and wild ponies. I recalled David Jones' delight in the legend that these were the descendants of the horses of Arthur's knights when they ran free after the defeat of the king and the end of Arthurian Britain. Now shrunk in size 'those straying riderless horses gone to grass in forest and on mountain, seem, as their masters, to have acquired a new yet aboriginal liberty'.[1] On the east, in contrast, lay a rolling landscape of low hills, and prosperous farms where neat hedgerows enclosed fields which were the result of the more fertile soil and the strength of the landowning families. Two differing worlds met here, each with its own past, shaped by geography, politics and people.

Through others' eyes

In the end, this border country and what it brings must remain elusive, like the mists and the ever-changing colours. It will speak to each of us differently, and it will say different things at different times. It will strike chords and bring glimpses – but it can never be possessed or fully understood.

Margiad Evans, a writer who spent some of the most formative years of her life in the Herefordshire border country claimed proudly, 'I am of the border, I belong to two worlds.' She lived first at Bridstow near Ross-on-Wye (as I also did in my teenage years) and then later at Langarron. She died quite young in 1958, far distant from the places that had meant so much to her. But in her autobiography and her journals she wrote about the effect that landscape had upon her. When she left it for good she said:

the memory is life-lasting; to move in this little-known land, only four miles from the Border at its nearest point, is . . . a complete fusion of Seeing and

Being. So that the way I walked, the garden I dug, was in some strange way myself thinking . . .[2]

Someone else, now a bishop on the other side of the country, also spent his earliest years on these borders and tells us that once he had left he never quite got over the acute sense of loss and of longing. Christopher Herbert, however, gives a timely warning about making too easy a connection between landscape and spirituality when he reminds us that:

There is something about the relationship between landscape and spirituality which is indefinable; and the relationship between spirituality and landscape on the borders is only glimpsed, never caught. It is the sight of the Black Mountains from Kings Thorne; . . . it is the twisting road . . . the sunlight . . . all those names which in their very structure tell us of their rounded quietness: Garway and Orcop, Much Marcle and Much Dewchurch.[3]

What R. S. Thomas says of his experience of North Wales, of the Lleyn peninsula where he lived for so much of his life, is equally true here. He also has a warning to those who are too quickly captivated by what they think they have found:

> You can come in
> You can come a long way . . .
> But you won't be inside.[4]

The poet Frances Horowitz, who knew and loved this countryside, lies buried at Orcop under the hill at Garway (strangely enough, two of the names in Christopher Herbert's list), in a grave that looks across to the Black Mountains. In one of her poems she remembers an afternoon spent at Capel-y-ffin, lying in the ferns beside the edge of a stream and listening to the hum of a bee. She tells us that, as she walked home through the mountain mist, 'the labyrinthine murmurings entered my mind'.[5]

This is such a personal experience that it is not surprising to find that the one thing all writers, whether of prose or of poetry, have in common is that they respect the way in which landscape opens up depths beyond itself. For one American poet it became a place of unveiling:

> On a glorious summer day
> this border country rolls out
> in a carpet of green turf,
> the fertile result
> of a blood-soaked history.
> A place where armies marched,
> kings were made and broken . . .

> Border lands often murmur
> of what was and might have been.
> God draws back the veil
> to make a Golden Valley
> between the Black Mountains,
> a place teeming with the life of
>   presence and past.[6]

Border or frontier?

I was fortunate that as I was thinking about this small
book not only did I have to break off and make visits
to London but I also went to spend three months in a
monastery in South Africa. This latter was particularly
significant for I found that I was now beginning to
ask myself questions: What is a frontier, a border, a
boundary, a threshold? A boundary gives a necessary
definition – a structure, a framework which one
respects. The whole monastic life shows us the vital role
of that – boundaries of time and place, held in a flexible
rhythm which ironically enough brings freedom (as it
does of course in the parallel situation of the family).
Boundaries, any good psychologist will tell us (and the
monastic tradition has an excellent grasp of psychologi-
cal insight) are very important and must be respected.
A frontier is designed to exclude the other. It is the
product of hostility, aggression, power. But my experience is of the Welsh Marches, neither boundary nor
frontier, but a borderland which marks (which is of

course where the old terms Marches or Marcher Lords originates) the point where the lands of two peoples run alongside one another. So I see borderlands as places where different cultures and histories meet and mix, perhaps challenge one another, and from which the new can then open up. And what I find in this outer landscape which is my home has also become true of the interior landscape, the inscape, which I cultivate and nurture.

In the eastern Cape in South Africa I saw a complete contrast in the way in which an imperial power had established frontiers to keep peoples apart. In order to push the Xhosa people back beyond the great Fish River, the British created a network of fortified positions along a line marked by palisades and forts, manned by constant patrols intended to maintain 'a proper degree of terror'. Here was a deliberate policy of creating barriers, in order to establish a clear demarcation line between cultural and racial difference of white and black by excluding and dividing. First written, as it were, on the soil itself in the nineteenth century, it was next to be carried over into legal, social and economic spheres in the twentieth century under the regime of apartheid. South Africa was now putting up the barricades, building bastions for people who were so completely and utterly sure of the rightness of their stance that they were shutting the doors physically and mentally on the other.

This is of course very little different from the many

frontiers through the world today. The one that runs between Arizona and Mexico is manned by US patrol vans in search of illegal immigrants, carrying the men who will raise a gun and ask *¿Qué estan haciendo aqui?* What are you doing here? Those attempting to cross a desert which is freezing in winter and infernally hot in summer are quite literally taking their lives into their hands in their desperate bid to escape their homeland, attempting to flee to a place which offers them no welcome. It is a story which can be repeated time and time again in a hundred different languages around the world.

A border priory

In the Welsh Marches I realised with gratitude that I belonged to another world. Both landscape and buildings gave me another message. St Mary's Priory in Monmouth, two or three miles from Tymawr, is a border place in every sense. It tells a wonderful story of how cultures and peoples have met and mingled here. We find a Benedictine priory built in Wales after the Norman conquest, a daughter house founded from a mother house in the Loire Valley, but also having a Breton involvement, which introduces a Celtic element. In the Preface to the history of the priory church Archbishop Rowan Williams explores the full significance of such a border situation:

This history gives us a good metaphor for a central aspect of Christian ministry. The priory built on a past legacy but moved in a new direction; it was founded by strangers who were also kindred. It is a 'border' place in every sense; and the future of the priory buildings must be about how that border is explored in such a way as to change strangers into kindred, and to bring people closer to that dangerous and transforming border between the world and God – the border that God himself upsets by his entry into the world on our terms, in flesh and blood.

Across the border, then, whether it's a human border or the strange frontier with God, is something or someone who is more hospitable than we dreamed; and we learn this by taking the risk of hospitality ourselves. Benedictine life if centred on God and on guests, seeing each in the other and learning from each how to relate to the other.[7]

INTERLUDE:

STANDING ON THE THRESHOLD

Rowan Williams tells us to take the risk of hospitality. When we turn to the Rule of St Benedict we are shown the fullness of what hospitality can mean. It is not merely the open door or the open gate which offers warmth, food, drink, but the open heart offering acceptance and love, and not least the open mind ready and willing to listen and to receive and exchange. St Benedict tells us to give a welcome to all who come because we see in them the figure of Christ himself. This means not judging or labelling, not being critical or competitive, or imprisoning the other in our demands and expectations. As so often, this is profound theological teaching presented in very down-to-earth and immediate terms. In Chapter 62 St Benedict describes the porter who stands at the gate of the monastery to exercise this art of hospitality on behalf of his brothers.

It is tender, funny and wise, a very simple but profound portrait, and we should not overlook its implications as a model for any of us. We see a man on the threshold, with one foot, as it were, in the monastic enclosure and the other in the world outside. Whenever anyone appears, he calls out his greeting 'Deo Gratias', Thank God you have come. It is a real welcome, of loving openness, and St Benedict uses two very simple phrases: 'all the gentleness that comes from the fear of God' and 'the warmth of love'.

In my own thinking and praying I have extended the image of the man on the margin to include greeting new circumstances, new situations and new demands so that even when they appear unexpectedly and I feel unready and ill prepared, I am yet prepared to welcome them. This image of being simultaneously firmly rooted and yet open, planted on either side of the threshold of the interior and the exterior, is one that I now want to apply elsewhere in my own personal experience.

2

TIMES AND SEASONS
OR CROSSING BETWEEN LIGHT
AND DARK

Place and time are the two primordial, inescapable realities which can either imprison or liberate us. How do we handle them? Even recognizing this and realising that it is our responsibility can be the first step to freedom. I find that I have been given an unexpected image in the medieval chained library of Hereford cathedral, and as the priest-poet David Scott reminds us, if we are thinking of heaven and earth, 'two major and distinct realities and you want to build some sort of bridge between them', then we can only deal in images which have always been a tool of writers for the exploration of truths.[1] In Hereford cathedral we find the Mappa Mundi, which is not a map in the usual sense at all but instead, in an apparently geographical map, gives us a picture of the medieval understanding of the world. Jerusalem is placed at the centre surrounded by countries and creatures, real and fantastical, which make up a total universe, real and imaginary, human and non-human, and in the triangular apex above the round world is Christ in Majesty presiding over it all, the work of his creation and redemption. We see God seated in glory and in judgement, inside and outside of time. And so here I am given an image of another border: that between time and eternity.[2]

For many of us time has become yet one more commodity of the consumer world, at the mercy of the dictates of deadlines and contracts, valued in terms of achievement and productivity. It is not easy to regain a sense of the changes of time and season when the night sky with all its gentle and subtle changes is blotted out by the sullen orange glow of the sodium light, denying us what should rightly be the timeless heritage of the movement of moon and stars. When the imported luxuries of the world stare us in the face on every visit to the supermarket, we are denied any sense of the coming and going of successive seasons of the year, with the expectation and delight that each will bring its own particular gift. If the kiwi fruits and the tomatoes and the strawberries are endlessly available, there is no longer that waiting on the threshold for each new season to bring its appropriate contribution of fruitfulness.

I have been discovering and incorporating into my own life the riches of the Celtic tradition and the Celtic way of looking at the world, with the result that I have found myself starting to see the year and to live it in the terms they did. It has brought a wonderfully vivid sense of time and season. Four days every year, each a festival with its particular associations and rituals, mark the transition from one season to the next. They become an invitation to be conscious of entering into something new, which will make new demands as well as bringing its own peculiar gifts. In America the Quaker theologian Parker Palmer was told about what to expect from an upper Mid-West winter: 'The winters will drive you crazy until you learn to *get out into them.*'[3] Here is the same encouragement to active engagement in what makes each season different.

The pattern of the day

Living on the borders brings me a very clear sense of the movement of time, of light and dark, of the changing seasons, and with it the underlying theme of death and life, darkness and light, creation and re-creation, which is inescapable for any of us, whether we live in an urban or a rural environment. For here we find ourselves touched by something primal, that repetition of birth and death, dying and new life, experienced again and again, year in year out, and repeated time and again throughout our lives.

Celtic peoples had rituals for every day and every season so that the passage of time was marked with due reverence and awareness. The day would start by saluting the rising sun, whom they hailed as they would a great person returning to their land. When the sun rose on the top of the peaks an old man in Arisaig

would put off his head-covering and would bow down
his head, giving glory to the great God of life for the
glory of the sun and for the goodness of its light to the
children of men and to the animals of the world.

> Hail to thee, thou sun of the seasons,
>> As thou traversest the skies aloft,
> Thy steps are strong on the wing of the heavens.[4]

Inside the house the woman lays the foundation of her
domestic duties by spreading the embers of the fire,
which has been burning throughout the night, in three
equal sections in a circle, laying a peat between them so
that each will touch the small boss in the middle which
forms the common centre. The first peat is laid down in
the name of the God of Life, the second the God of
Peace, the third the God of Grace and the circle is then
covered in the name of the Three of Light. Fire, light,
warmth – the image of the nurturing and sustaining
hand of God and of the need for these same qualities
within our own selves, is here enacted as a daily ritual.
This can easily seem romantic and distant, far removed
from the technology of the electric switch, the electric
coffee-maker, the electric kettle, or whatever forms the
first ritual of bringing warmth into the start of our day.
And yet the reality of doing an action with awareness,
consciousness of the presence of God, gratitude for his
gifts of power or water or light, still remains the same.
An action performed consciously and with reverence

gives meaning to the start of the day and thus to a hallowing of time and its handling with care.

This daily celebration of the coming of the light of each day then became in the Celtic tradition a daily reminder of heaven, of the future light of eternity:

O God, who broughtest me from the rest of last night
Unto the joyous light of this day,
Be Thou bringing me from the new light of this day
Unto the guiding light of eternity.
    Oh! from the new light of this day
    Unto the guiding light of eternity.

Then there is a prayer in the evening, as the light fades at dusk, at the time of 'the change-over routine' as naturalists in Africa call that moment when evening falls and the wild creatures welcome the coming of the darkness:

I am in hope, in its proper time,
That the great and gracious God
Will not put out for me the light of grace
    Even as thou dost leave me this night.

This is a reminder of something which it is only too easy to forget in a culture of urban values: both the light and the dark sustain us. 'There is a place within the providence of God for the darkness, the night, the shadow,' John Davies writes.

Our individual formation is in the dark, between
conception and birth. The mysterious workings of
our bodies are in the dark. The seed grows secretly in
the dark. . . . We need to recognise and work with
this darkness, even when we feel that it is opposing
the light which is the primary gift of God.'[5]

'Darkness and light are both alike to Thee' sings
the psalmist, and just as we can learn so much from the
songs of the people of Israel, so we also learn from
the songs that were always in the hearts and on the lips
of the Celtic peoples. They make me conscious of what
otherwise I might easily neglect, those crossing-over
moments which carry me between the dark and the
light, the light and the dark, taking me daily and yearly
from one to the other. As George Mackay Brown
reminds us, they knew of the Light behind the light
which gives life and meaning to all the creatures of
earth:[6]

> The eye of the great God
> The eye of the God of glory,
> The eye of the King of hosts,
> The eye of the King of the living,
>   Pouring upon us
>   At each time and season
>   Pouring upon us
>   Gently and generously.[7]

There are so many prayers throughout the ages on this theme of the celebration of the coming of the light – the light that is the dawn, that is the light of life, that is Christ himself. I end this section with one that I have taken from Bede so that if we turn to the Celtic tradition we do not forget the riches of the Anglo-Saxon world:

> Grant us your light, O Lord,
> that the darkness in our hearts
> being wholly passed away,
> we may come at last to the light
> which is Christ.
> For Christ is the morning star,
> who when the night of this world has passed,
> brings to us
> the promised light of life,
> and opens to them eternal day. Amen.[8]

Praying the seasons

As the sun passed through its four stations during a year, the equinoxes and the solstices became significant moments in the Celtic year. They were celebrated as a succession of threshold moments, each with its name and its rituals to carry men and women on into the next season. The year began at Samhaine on 1st November. Country folk around me still speak of this as 'the turning of the year', and for many people, whether they celebrate the pre-Christian Samhaine or the Christian

24

feasts of All Saints and All Souls, this is the thinnest time of the year, the time at which the veil between time and eternity can easily become transparent. With the drawing in of the days, the coming of darkness, and the prospect of winter with all its attendant hardships and ills, it was the time to bring the flocks down from their summer pastures, and those animals which could not be kept would be slaughtered and their carcasses and bones burnt, in bonfires. It was as if, George Mackay Brown tells us, 'the children of the sun were entreating the light to return from darkness, to stay with them, to provide them with corn and milk and fleeces through the lessening days of autumn and winter'.[9] The landscape becomes bare, stripped, cold, stark, dead.

Can we still find significance in the passing of the seasons? Can we live into them in such a way that we allow their changes to shape the pattern of our prayer? It is undoubtedly easier in a place where I can watch the moon wax and wane, see the stars move across the horizon, see the trees gain and lose their foliage, and notice the gradual shading of the colours around me. To begin the year with the drawing in of the days from 1st November, which I have now begun to do, has become very important and very powerful in my own life. It must inevitably take a different form in a town, but if you look you can still find the images which encourage turning the cycle of the seasons into reflective praying.

Fr Philip Jebb, OSB Prior of the Benedictine Abbey of Downside, has given us his own response:

Winter has a message all its own;
. . .
The trees are naked, without leaves or flowers or fruit;
But the bare branches give us glimpses of the stars;
They reach their fingers to heaven,
Even as their roots hold fast to the earth.
Linked by the strong trunk, giving interchange of life,
symbols of our dual nature and inheritance.[10]

Spring comes with the feast of Imbolc on 1st February, (which is also the feast of St Brigid, and the following day is Candlemas). This was the time of the lactation of the ewes, and for those of us in the northern hemisphere the moment when the first shoots of new growth start to break through the dark soil, drawn by the promise of the sunlight.

We breathe a new air,
No longer cold with seeming death.
The flowers respond
    to the strengthening Sun, your light.
So may our hearts respond to your love and grace.
The birds break into song and call us to your praise.
So may our hearts give praise at all aspects of our lives.
The frozen earth and water melt to new life:
So may our hardened hearts be softened
    to gentleness and love.
We are overwhelmed with images, symbols,
confirmations of your resurrecting, your enlivening.

The year is swinging on its pivot, and bringing us to the start of summer, celebrated on 1st May as the feast of Beltaine. Now that the light begins to overtake the dark, the days lengthen and nights are shorter. It was the time when the flocks would be taken from their winter quarters to graze and fatten in the high meadows throughout the summer. The people moved with their animals so that there was a regular transition and the farm names *hendre* and *hafod* found throughout the area refer to these winter and summer farms respectively, so that the landscape still carries a reminder of the yearly pattern of transition.

If Imbolc is the season of light Beltaine is the season of growth, and prayer becomes praise for fulfilment:

> Strong image of your creative power.
> Calling forth the endless variety of your creative
>   imagination:
> Colour, scent and sound.
> Making for Beauty
> And for peaceful Joy.

Finally, on 1st August the feast of Lammas marks the beginning of the harvest when the earth brings its fruits to birth. Because of the new pattern of the year dictated to us by school terms and holidays which cut across the older and more natural rhythms of the seasons, the common assumption is to regard August as the height of summer, the time for seaside holidays, camping, journeys abroad. But I have found that to follow the Celtic sense of timing now feels much more convincing. For this is harvest time, the gathering in of the fruits, the time to celebrate the main subsistence crops, whether of the fields, the hedgerows or the orchards – and not least the time for their storing, conserving and preserving in whatever way is the most appropriate to each. Sadly, for many today, this is disappearing, for the speed at which we live and the ease of frozen food have meant the loss of those earlier traditional skills which respected the unique character and quality of each thing as it came to ripen and be gathered and handled accordingly.

The Orthodox liturgy of the Transfiguration on 6th August ends with the blessing of the first fruits. This should be one of the most joyous of times because the threshold of plenty has been crossed. So Philip Jebb prays:

> The flowers have turned to seeds and fruit,
> For our enjoyment,
> Our sustenance,
> And our future life.
> This is the time of fulfilment and completion.
> It had a beauty of its own:
> Perfect symbol of your providence.
> We rejoice in the fruits you give us
> in your loving generosity.

INTERLUDE:

THE RITUAL OF THE THRESHOLD

Each season has its special character, its gifts, its differences in the play of light and dark. Much of its richness comes from the conscious crossing of the border between one season and the next. The Celtic year rejoices in this succession of thresholds of celebration, ritual, prayer and praise. Here is a living out of that wise old saying of Porphyrus, 'A threshold is a sacred thing.' I experienced this in Japan in a daily context. The custom was, before entering a house, a person stands at the entrance, removes their shoes, and on crossing the lintel into the interior puts on other slippers. It showed me the handling of time and space in a deliberate and conscious way: taking time to stand still, even if only for a moment; the respect for space; the encounter between the exterior and the interior.

In the old days there used to be the practice in monastic communities of *statio*: again, it is the recognition of the threshold moment. The monk or nun will enter the church with time to stand, to wait, to let go of the previous activity with all its concurrent anxieties and demands and in a moment of stillness enter instead into the space kept open for the Word. By rushing into the saying of the office, as a matter of duty or obligation, without that pause, a few extra moments may be gained for work, but what is lost is the awareness and attention that mean being totally present, crossing over into the time and space for the *opus Dei*, the work of God.

3

EMBRACING LIFE'S CHANGES

From birth to death

Can this theme of crossing the borders apply to the pattern of my own life? What about all those transitions that occur from birth to death? They are not generally marked by ritual apart from the three events for which today's society has fashionable social (and religious) gatherings: baptism, marriage and death. Christenings, weddings and funerals are ceremonies which reflect important public high moments, and this is absolutely right. But they do not help when I feel the need for something in addition, for some ritual which will recognize that in all our lives there are a succession of passing-over moments, many of which must remain secret and private.

The traditional world-view, entrenched into every African child's psyche, speaks of inter-related worlds, the world of the living and the world of the dead, together making one whole and complete community under God's direct control and influence. They belong to these two worlds which overlap and inter-connect. They never forget the spirit world, the human being as part of a bigger system. They see earth as a gift from God, the rendezvous of the dead and the living. They speak to us of what is fundamental, universal, and which all of us recognize as being part of that primal vision – to which we are heir – even though sometimes we have neglected it, and with God's grace need to reclaim.

In the *Carmina Gadelica* we see how until quite recently life in the Scottish highlands and islands had its rituals and blessings for every stage of the life of the household and family members conducted in the home itself. From the moment of birth the mother would make a distinction between the more formal clerical or great baptism in church and the birth baptism over which she presided in the house.

The new-born child would be passed three times across the hearth and then carried three times sun-wise round the hearth, ensuring its insertion into the natural rhythm and flow of the universe, and then finally three drops of water would be placed on its head. Here are timeless, primal elements, powerful images which transcend our immediate experience.

Coming of age

I was reminded of just how powerful such rituals can, and perhaps should be, from my experience of Africa. While I was staying in the monastery a young man was going through the traditional initiation rites which mark the transition to manhood. He was in his hut on the edge of the property, and although of course I did not see him – all women are rigidly excluded during this time – I knew what was happening.

Customs and tradition are firmly established in Xhosa tribal life so that as a person moves from childhood to teenager to adult to middle age and finally to old age each step has its dress, its songs and dances. They believe that this age grouping brings stability to the social structure and establishes a succession of responsibilities and obligations. What was happening on the hillside was the initiation rite into manhood of this young *umkhetha* which was essentially based on circumcision, and involved exclusion from all tribal life until the cut healed. Then the young men would emerge with new clothes (particularly noticeable were their tweed caps) and with white clay on their faces in public demonstration of their new status in society. Although this may seem far from any western experience it gave me a powerful image. Wrapped only in a blanket and in the simplicity of a hut specially built of branches which will later be burned, this time of initiation requires poverty and nakedness, or near nakedness. There is a sense of being re-born, divesting oneself, becoming a *tabula rasa* ready to be filled with the knowledge and wisdom of the tribe. It seemed to me that there was a parallel here with the novice, who on admission to the community lies prostrate on the ground, saying *Suscipe me*, accept me, receive me, here I am before God empty in order to receive.

33

There is this same almost physical quality in the blessing that the mother would give to the son or daughter who was leaving home:

> Be the great God between thy two shoulders
> To protect thee in thy going and in thy coming.

A ritual for letting a son or daughter go free, handing them over, under the protection of God, is not anything that we naturally include as a part of growing up, and yet again it shows us one of the most important steps of all of the transitions in life if anyone is to move on into freedom and maturity from the confines of the family.

Death

As the time of death draws closer there is this same sense of confidence in the abiding presence of a God who is alongside us and has walked every step of the way with us. There is therefore nothing at all remote or abstract in the blessings that are asked before 'crossing the black river of death; the great oceans of darkness; and the mountains of eternity'. For while a funeral is an event shared by family and friends, the time of dying is uniquely personal. Keeping watch beside the bedside of an old woman as she was dying I found, as I said them time and again, that these deathbed blessings had a sense of being outside of time, and their constant repetition enhanced their timeless quality. Many, as this

one, have a strong sense of passage, and although ultimately that passing over from this life is made alone,
those who have preceded us, the saints and the angels,
are waiting to bring us to God.

> Be each saint in heaven,
> Each sainted woman in heaven,
> each angel in heaven
> Stretching their arms for you,
> Smoothing the way for you,
> When you go thither
>   Over the river hard to see;
> Oh when you go thither home
>   Over the river hard to see.

If we begin to see the world in this way, then nightfall
and sleep become a nightly reminder of that final crossing over, which will in the end bring us from sleep and
death into light and life.

> Be this soul on Thine arm, O Christ,
> Thou King of the City of Heaven.

Embracing change

If we are going to see life as a succession of thresholds to
be crossed, it recalls the journeys of the people of Israel
in the desert, and gives us symbols and images which
we can apply to our own experience. The very words

'passover' or 'exodus' carry a fullness of meaning as a journey from bondage into freedom. It is important to remember that the ritual of the passover was a yearly ritual, so that memory was kept alive and the cycle lived through time and time again:

> As we sing our own song of Freedom by practising the Art of Passingover ... gradually the face of our life begins to change; it becomes face of freedom.[1]

The psalms are the journey songs of the people who made that journey, and if we try to sanitize, edit, or sentimentalize them they lose their power. They are the songs of a people who are moving away from a known situation into the unknown, and often they are very angry with a God who removes all those certainties, and instead seems to be leading them along a very precarious path. They do not sit down for long beside gently flowing streams or linger in lush meadows. When we pray the psalms as they did, we too are compelled to stay 'at the raw edge', in the words of Walter Brueggemann.[2]

In the Gospels we watch a Christ who in dismissing certainties shows us what freedom might mean. We watch the way in which he enters into people's lives and *dissolves* an existing situation, whatever it might be. The likelihood was that it had promised security, safety, and now instead people are being challenged to *leave* their nets, or to *leave* a nice safe booth, and instead to follow him. Christ says to Peter, James and John 'Come', and to Matthew 'Stand up, move, walk, come with me'. Our God is a God who moves and he invites us to move with him. He wants to pry us away from anything that might hold us too securely, our careers, our family systems, our money making. We must be ready to disconnect. There comes a time when the things which were undoubtedly good and right in the past must be left behind, for there is always the danger that they might hinder us from moving forward and connecting with the one thing necessary, Christ himself.

When Brueggemann is writing about the Jewish people at one historic point in their story, the sacking of Jerusalem and the loss of the temple in 597, he uses the word *relinquish*.[3] It becomes a metaphor for the opening up to the new gifts and new forms of life given by God which become possible just when everything seems to have come to an end. Of course there is loss and it is right to grieve and not to pretend otherwise. Insecurity makes certitude attractive, and it is in times like these that I want to harness God to my preferred scheme of things, for it is risky to be so vulnerable. Yet it is just this which asks for trust and hope in God's plans, not mine. So I try to learn each time that I am called upon to move forward to try to hand over the past freely, putting it behind me and moving on with hands open and ready for the new.

In the garden Christ gently but deliberately says to Mary Magdalene '*Noli me tangere*'. 'Do not touch' is a misleading translation which deprives us of the significance of what is happening here. 'Do not cling' is a more accurate rendering of the Greek, for surely we do need to touch, to touch the hem of the garment, to touch the wounds and feel them. But we must not *cling*, for that carries the danger of becoming dependent, of clutching or holding on in the wrong way. I love that statue by Elisabeth Frink in the cathedral close at Salisbury, of the walking Madonna. Here is this young woman who strides out boldly into the future, her one hand strong and determined, while the other is vulnerable. She knows that she has seen the Lord, the risen Christ, she has heard the resurrection message and now she is ready to cross the threshold and to engage with whatever lies before her.

What gives her the strength to move forward with such assurance, calling out that loving welcome, that *Deo Gratias*, to a future which is unsure, unknown?

INTERLUDE:

CROSSING OVER WITH
SAINTS AND ANGELS

The barriers go down between this world and the next. Celtic blessings and rituals carry the African sense of 'the living dead'. I know no better expression of this than in the poem of a twentieth-century Welsh poet writing of the presence of St David on the soil of Wales today:

> There is no barrier between two worlds in the Church,
> The Church militant on earth
> Is one with the Church triumphant in heaven,
> And the saints are in this Church which is two in one.[1]

The saints accompany us on our journeys. The angels move easily between heaven and earth. There is constant crossing between two worlds. 'A hill touches an angel' in the words of Dylan Thomas, a Welsh poet *par excellence*, and there are more attributions to St Michael with all his angels in this area than in the rest of the country. Bucolic angels smile from tombstones in the churchyard or look down on us from funerary tablets on the walls of churches as we sit in the pew below them. In the priory church at Abergavenny the giant wooden figure of Jesse lies on his side while the angel at his head keeps watch:

> The angel at his head is awake to see for him . . .
> Jesse need not wake yet With amazement, the angel sees.[2]

The Revd Francis Kilvert, the nineteenth-century country parson and diarist living here in the Welsh borders, came to know his people and their local traditions well. In one of his parishes he was told that the people used to gather on Easter morning 'to see the sun dance and play in the water and the angels who were at the Resurrection playing backwards and forwards before the sun'. They were not serving any useful purpose as Ruth Bidgood tells us in her poem 'Resurrection Angels', they were not there for healing, they were at play – and their dancing and playing touched something in each of the onlookers:

> To and fro went the wings, to and fro
> over the water, playing before the sun.
> . . .
> The people had no words to tell
> the astonishment, the individual bounty –
> for each his own dance in the veins,
> brush of wings on the soul.[3]

4

CONNECTING INNER
AND OUTER

The inner cloisters

In his book *Living on the Border of the Holy*, a title which is in itself significant, William Countryman writes of that border country which we all carry within us. He describes it as a kind of fault line which runs right down the middle of our lives. We can of course ignore it but it does not go away. We all live with it and we all have our unique experience of it, for it is part of who we are as human beings. It connects the surface or the ordinary reality with its deeper roots, indeed, he would actually claim that the border country is the realm in which human existence finds its meaning:

> This border country is a place of intense vitality. It does not so much draw us away from the everyday world as it plunges us deeper into a reality of which the everyday world is like the surface . . .
>
> To live there for a while is like having veils pulled away. In the long run we find that the border country is in fact the place we have always lived, but it is seen

in a new and clearer light. Stay at the border, in active conversation with the holy and the everyday.[1]

If we now return to St Benedict's portrait of the porter waiting at the gates, we could almost say that this shows us a conversation between the holy and the everyday – between the inner enclosure with its life of prayer and the exterior world with all its distractions and demands. How do we hold the two together? How do we have a conversation and not a confrontation? He shows us what makes possible this strong, warm act of welcome. We see this figure of *stability*, someone who does not go wandering off, either literally or metaphorically. He is firmly rooted in this place, in himself. It is from this firm internal centre that the external can be greeted and welcomed, however strange, even challenging, it might appear. The porter gives us the image of standing on the threshold between two worlds.

The demands of the enclosure, with its times of prayer and silence, ask for those qualities of commitment and continuity, which bring a strong underpinning not only to the Benedictine life but to any fulfilled and balanced life. In the cloister we have such an amazing image, that I return to it time and again. What other complex of buildings has the audacity to put emptiness at its heart? It originated in the eighth century when the cloister and the church were established as the two essential elements of the monastic buildings. Since then it has taken many forms and variants, as in Namibia where the Tutsing

Missionary Benedictine sisters have just built a cloister whose walkways open out at each of the four corners so that the community should never feel separated from the mountainside on which the monastery is built. To walk slowly around these four sides, whether they were built in Africa in the twenty-first century or in France in the Middle Ages, can tell us so much about how emptiness and stillness at the heart of life can be achieved.

So these passageways play a practical purpose which is also symbolic. They link up all those buildings which serve the daily needs of a life which recognizes the demands of body, mind and spirit – the holding together of the physical self with its need for sleep and food (the dormitory and the refectory); the self of the mind (the library where the intellect comes into play and the chapter house where matters of day-to-day administration, finance and business are handled, requiring the use of the intelligence); and finally the spiritual self (the church or the oratory). In the end, one might say that this whole balance of the three elements is actually dependent on the church, for it is the time and place for prayer which is the one essential priority that anchors everything else. Sleeping, eating, studying, manual work, decision-making – all these other activities flow in and out of the work of God, the *opus Dei*. Prayer is the unifying foundation that maintains everything else in equilibrium. Muddle, confusion, being pulled first in one direction and then another, militate against a life with any sense of rhythm or unity. But here we see how living, however busy daily work may be, and praying, can now become one continuous flowing movement so that life becomes whole, a unified whole, in which no one thing is set above another.

Around that central open space run the arches, the succession of columns or pillars which carry round the inner sides of the cloister walkways. Constantly changing according to the times of the day, the seasons of the year, they present us with a variety of amazingly varied and beautiful shadow patterns. Without these shadows would there be the same perspective? That is a good question to ask. It brings me back to the earlier theme of the light and the dark and the interplay of the two.

A gardener who travelled widely to write a book on monastic gardens was struck by the cloister garth, or garden, this central space, open to the heavens, funnelling daylight into the heart of the monastery. He noticed how often members of a community liked to sit in the cloister at twilight, reading by the last rays of daylight before Compline, and reflected on the importance of the presence of light together with the presence of the green of grass and flowers, and above all the fountain or spring which brings a quiet and continuous undercurrent of sound to the whole.

Living in a building with good light is mentally uplifting . . . The setting of green grass within the cloister range has long been known to have a unique power

and grace and to exert a kind of subliminal attrac-
tion ... cloister garths create green oases of safety,
simplicity, and purity.[2]

As I apply these comments to my own inner self, I am
reminded of the need to keep a garden watered and
fresh throughout all the differing times of the day and
the changing seasons of the year. But it is the water in
the centre which furnishes the most significant image.
For it is the refreshment of the spring of living water
which keeps the garden green and gives it life.

Passing over and coming back

There are so many ways of describing this still centre:
the cave of the heart, the hidden *poustinia*, the inner-
most cloister. Each one of us has our own picture.
Essentially it is that deep place where God finds us and
we find him. It is not empty space *per se*; its purpose is
to become the space for listening to the Word. We enter
into silence and hear God's conversation and take our
proper part in it – and if we heed ancient wisdom, that
means trying not to say too much ourselves.

But it is the centre from which we move outwards.
Monastic men and women, Thomas Merton above all,
describe themselves as people who are marginal, who
are living on the edges, and yet they are also the most
profoundly centred. As I think about the centre and the
edges in my own life I ask myself about the relationship

of the two. Are the edges not perhaps the centre? Does the centre not hold the edges? Perhaps it is just simply finding the right connection of the two, the right way of coming and going.

If the borders are not frontiers, and if the thresholds are continually crossed and re-crossed, then we open up to the new. John Dunne reminds us that: 'We all have this capacity to pass over and to come back again to ourselves, but we do not all discover it or learn how to use it.' He then goes on to say: 'I feel able to pass over into the other and come back again with new insights to my own.'[3]

Encountering new worlds

At the very end of his Rule when St Benedict encourages his followers, in an almost throw-away line, to continue reading and studying, he then goes on to make suggestions about what he would like them to study. It is one of the best examples of being told about being ready to open up to the new. For the two main sources which he proposes are taken from almost diametrically opposing perspectives, very different in their approach. To explore divergent forms of monastic experience was not going to be a comfortable exercise. Yet the man who is looking for the welcome of the open door and the open heart is also looking for the open mind. The porter who welcomes the stranger, the visiting monk, and the brothers who take him in, are also ready to

listen to him. It may well be that this man comes from some different tradition, but they accept that he has something to say from which they will learn. To listen to everyone, whoever they may be, brother, child, stranger, is important. I like to think of this exchange as conversation; it is gentler than the word dialogue, which often carries a sense of confrontation. *A Vow of Conversation* is the title which Thomas Merton gave to his Journals for the years 1964–65 and in his case it becomes a play on words.[4] He is referring to *conversatio morum*, the vow of conversion of manners, to continual conversion and ongoing transformation in the life of a Trappist monk. But it also describes the way in which this solitary hermit loved to receive that stream of visitors who came from all walks of life and every sort of religious, philosophical, literary background to talk with him and exchange ideas. His vow of stability had brought him rootedness both in the Trappist community at Gethsemani and also more profoundly in his own inner self. It gave him the place from which his interior journey could begin – breaking open new worlds, asking new questions, unveiling new vistas.[5] In the last year of his life he wrote of the need for effort, deepening, change and transformation. Not that I must undertake a special project of self-transformation or that I must 'work on myself . . . let change come quietly and invisibly on the inside'.[6]

Finale

I have been writing this book at my cottage in the Welsh borders during the summer months, hoping to finish it by Lammas. I have gone constantly from my study to the orchard, the copse, the riverbank, taking with me my half-resolved thinking, and letting the rhythm between house and garden, inside and outside, work on me. Gardening in itself has about it something of this art of conversation. For my garden only exists through the 'conversation' between myself and the given quality of the land itself in its natural state. I try to respect and enhance this without dominating. I try to do enough clearing, letting in of the light and removing the destructive forces, to allow a continual exchange between myself and the natural elements. I hope that from this will emerge something that reflects a partnership between us. And since it is changing all the time, not only throughout the seasons but also year by year, as old trees die or floods alter the shape of the banks, it will continue as an ongoing conversation in which both of us are involved. It is itself a reminder of border life.

Just as there is something unpredictable in living beside a stream, which continuously changes shape and configuration, so I come to the end of this exploration of the image of the border to accept that it will not conclude with any clear-cut picture. When I return to the post-apartheid South Africa I find a contrast between those years, terrible as they were, when people felt that

they knew where they stood on issues which seemed clear-cut, and the present situation which appears so much more confused and volatile. It was simpler then, living comfortably in a white suburb and not venturing out into what lay beyond, in the other world of the townships. The grandson of William Verwoerd, now a member of the ANC, uses the word 'ambiguous' and says that we have to learn to live with ambiguity. Certainty can appear immensely attractive, appealing both to individuals and to nations above all in times of suffering and distress. Complexity, ambiguity, untidiness – these are very different, and I have come to find that they carry more conviction. The closed mind, the *laager* mentality, is the greatest obstacle to any real freedom – the freedom of openness. As soon as we admit that there are no right answers, that we must be ready to live with contradiction, we are forced instead to listen to one another, to admit our need to learn, to recognize our need to receive.

let us live with uncertainty
as with a friend
to feel certain
means feeling secure.
To feel safe is unreal,
a delusion of self
knowing we do not know is
the only certainty letting the self be lost into Christ.

These words which were written anonymously by a monastic, speak of the courage and strength that come from this way of living. It may be a brave, even a fool-hardy or risky undertaking, but if we choose to live on the borders we find ourselves part of a company of fellow-travellers who are ready to say:

> For us there are no certainties, no star
> blazing our journey, . . .
>   We try
> out our way lit with angels, wondering
> 'How far?'[7]

Perhaps there is something prophetic about living on the border. I want a Christianity which brings me comfort, but also dis-comfort. Walter Brueggemann said that borders were not safe places since one finds oneself driven to the 'raw edges' of humanness. In the new science I find a vocabulary which, even if I do not fully understand it, helps me to articulate my own thoughts.[8] The old world of Newtonian certainty drew lines and was happy with whatever was systematic, rational, and could be subjected to reason. Now in a world of inter-relatedness 'connections work across the separations'. 'Senders and receivers' are linked together in a way that means energy, fertility, new birth. This is inevitably more complex and more demanding, just when I would like things to become smoother and simpler. Listening to the voices asks me to be attentive

to the place where I stand but also to ask questions of myself and to be open and willing to recognize where the other might bring in a corrective, a deepening or strengthening. Perhaps this will be painful, opening up areas of consciousness that previously were dormant. But in a two-way exchange the other has as much to give as I have to receive. Ideally the border should be the image of encounter and contrast can lead, not to syncretism, but to a moving forward in greater fullness. It is an image which church and society have needed more. God, who is there at the centre, is also at the raw edges, the living God who will not let us settle easily or for too long . . . Our God is too big for either/or. Instead both / and will take us into the realm of paradox, where we meet our God who is both known and unknown.

NOTES

Introduction

1. L. William Countryman, *Forgiven and Forgiving*, Morehouse Publishing, Harnsberg, PA 1998, pp. 1–2.
2. Paul Hill, 'The Art of David Jones' in *David Jones*, London, Tate Gallery Publications Department, 1991, p. 24.

1. The Border Landscape

1. David Jones, *Epoch and Artist*, London, Faber, 1959, p. 251.
2. Moira Dearnley, *Margiad Evans*, Cardiff, University of Wales Press, on behalf of the Welsh Arts Council, 1982, p. 62. Her *Autobiography*, originally written in 1943, was reprinted again in revised form in 1974 (London, Calder & Boyars). See also the new edition of *The Old and the Young*, (Seren Bridgend, mid-Glamorgan) re-published by Seren, Poetry of Wales Press, in 1998 with introduction and notes by Ceridwen Lloyd-Morgan.
3. Christopher Herbert, Bishop of St Albans, preaching

at the Friends of Hereford Cathedral Festival Service, June 1998, reprinted in *The Sixty Fifth Annual Report*, pp. 10–13.

4. R. S. Thomas, *Collected Poems 1945–1990*, Phoenix, London, 1993, p. 207. Permission sought.
5. Frances Horowitz, *Collected Poems*, Newcastle Upon-Tyne, Bloodaxe Books, 1985, p. 74.
6. Bonnie Thurston, *The Heart's Lands*, Abergavenny, Three Peaks Press, 2001, p. 33. Professor Thurston has lectured in theology for twenty-five years and written widely on New Testament studies. This poem – and others on Herefordshire – are the result of time spent here on the borders. Permission sought.
7. *A History of the Benedictine Priory of the Blessed Virgin Mary and St Florent at Monmouth*, Aberystwyth, Cambrian Printers, 2001.

2 Times and Seasons

1. David Scott, *Sacred Tongues, The Golden Age of Spiritual Writing*, London, SPCK, 2001, p. 6.
2. There is now a great deal of interesting material on the map. The best short introduction is that of Meryl Jancy, *Mappa Mundi: A Brief Guide*, Hereford, Hereford Cathedral Enterprises, 1995.
3. Quoted from Parker Palmer. Source unknown.
4. I have taken all the quotations that follow from my own editing of the *Carmina Gadelica*, in *The Celtic*

Vision, Prayers and Blessings from the Outer Hebrides, London, Darton, Longman & Todd, latest edition 2001, or the new edition from Ligouri Publications, Missouri, 2001.

5. John Davies, *God at Work, Creation Then and Now: A Practical Exploration*, London, Canterbury Press, 2001, p. 12.

6. A phrase from George Mackay Brown in an introduction to his poems written in December 1995. Source unknown.

7. Quoted from George Mackay Brown. Source unknown.

8. Douglas Dales, *Christ the Golden-Blossom: A Treasury of Anglo-Saxon Prayer*, London, Canterbury Press, 2001, p. 17.

9. Quoted from George Mackay Brown. Source unknown.

10. Brigid Boardman and Philip Jebb, *In a Quiet Garden. Meditations and Prayerful Reflections*, Stratton on the Fosse, Downside Abbey Books, Bath. All the quotations that I have used in this section are taken from the section on the seasons, pp. 82–8. Quoted with permission.

3 Embracing Life's Changes

1. Francis Duff, *The Art of Passingover*, New York, Paulist Press, 1988, p. 153.

2. Walter Brueggemann, *Hopeful Imagination: Pro-*

phetic Voices in Exile, Philadelphia, Fortress Press, 1986.

3. D. Gwenallt Jones, *St David*. For the full text see *Threshold of Light, Prayers and Praises from the Celtic Tradition*, ed. A. M. Allchin, and Esther de Waal, London, Darton, Longman & Todd, 1990, pp. 39–41. *Daily Readings from Prayers and Praises in the Celtic Tradition*, Springfield, Illinois, Templegate Publishers, 1986.

Interlude: Crossing over with Saints and Angels

1. Ruth Bidgood, *Singing to Wolves*, Seren, Poetry Wales Press, 2000, p. 29. Quoted with permission.
2. Ruth Bidgood, *Selected Poems*, Seren, Poetry of Wales Press, 1992, p. 34. Quoted with permission.
3. Ibid.

4 Connecting Inner and Outer

1. L. William Countryman, *Living on the Border of the Holy: The Human Priesthood and the Church*, Harrisburg, Pennsylvania, Morehouse Publishing, 1999.
2. Mick Hales, *Monastic Gardens*, New York, Stewart, Tabori & Chang, 2000, Chapter 1, The Cloister Garth, pp. 14–30.
3. John Dunne, *The House of Wisdom*, London, SCM Press, 1985.

4. The art of conversation is not only gentler but it is an art which can be learned. I am grateful to William Countryman for clarification on this small but important point who in a few sentences helped to put my own experience into clearer perspective, op. cit., p. 205, note 27; p. 204, note 26. *A Vow of Conversation* was published in Basingstoke, England by the Lamp Press in 1988.
5. Thomas Merton, *Woods, Shore, Desert: A Notebook May 1968*, Santa Fe, Museum of New Mexico Press, 1982.
6. Ibid., p. 48.
7. Sr Jennifer Dines, Order of Augustinian Canonesses, and lecturer at Heythrop College, London.
8. I have gained much from reading Margaret Wheatley, *Leadership and the New Science*, p. 28.